THE PRAYER JOURNAL

6 Month Journal for Prayer,
Gratitude and Connection with God

This Journal belongs to:

_____

ISBN-10: 1721094903
ISBN-13: 978-1721094905
Limits of Liability and Disclaimer of Warranty
The author and publisher shall not be liable for your misuse of this material.
This book is strictly for informational and educational purposes.

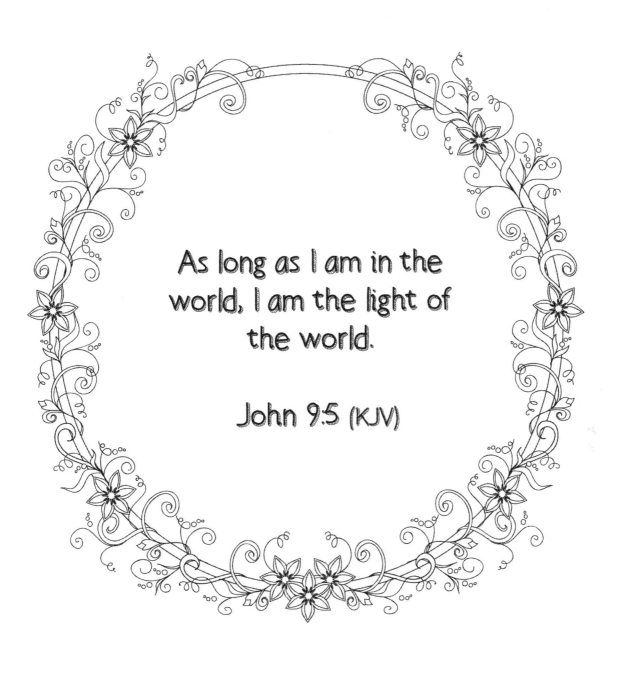

As long as I am in the
world, I am the light of
the world.

John 9:5 (KJV)

Date: 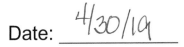 4/30/19

Today's Bible verse:

People in need of Prayer:

Mary - Ellen's
sister and family
Zach Lynch - healing
+ success
Kyle - summer work
Melissa's mom
Bonnie's mom

Prayer Requests:

Short term:

a good day of
fasting, patience

Long term:

Patience
and discipline

Thank you Lord for:

my husband + son
my upbringing
my faith

Today I learned:

_____
_____
_____

Date: _____

Today's Bible verse:

People in need of Prayer:

Prayer Requests:

Short term:

Long term:

Thank you Lord for:

Today I learned:

_____

_____

_____

Date: _____

Today's Bible verse:

People in need of Prayer:

Prayer Requests:

Short term:

Long term:

Thank you Lord for:

Today I learned:

_____

_____

_____

Date: _____

Today's Bible verse:

People in need of Prayer:

Prayer Requests:

Short term:

Long term:

Thank you Lord for:

Today I learned:

_____

_____

_____

Date: _____

Today's Bible verse:

People in need of Prayer:

Prayer Requests:

Short term:

Long term:

Thank you Lord for:

Today I learned:

_____

_____

_____

Date: _____

Today's Bible verse:

People in need of Prayer:

Prayer Requests:

Short term:

Long term:

Thank you Lord for:

Today I learned:

_____

_____

_____

Date: _____

Today's Bible verse:

People in need of Prayer:

Prayer Requests:

Short term:

Long term:

Thank you Lord for:

Today I learned:

_____
_____
_____

Date: _____

Today's Bible verse:

People in need of Prayer:

Prayer Requests:

Short term:

Long term:

Thank you Lord for:

Today I learned:

_____

_____

_____

Date: _____

Today's Bible verse:

People in need of Prayer:

Prayer Requests:

Short term:

Long term:

Thank you Lord for:

Today I learned:

_____

_____

_____

Date: _____

Today's Bible verse:

People in need of Prayer:

Prayer Requests:

Short term:

Long term:

Thank you Lord for:

Today I learned:

_____

_____

_____

Date: _____

Today's Bible verse:

People in need of Prayer:

Prayer Requests:

Short term:

Long term:

Thank you Lord for:

Today I learned:

_____

_____

_____

Date: _____

Today's Bible verse:

People in need of Prayer:

Prayer Requests:

Short term:

Long term:

Thank you Lord for:

Today I learned:

_____
_____
_____

Date: _____

Today's Bible verse:

People in need of Prayer:

Prayer Requests:

Short term:

Long term:

Thank you Lord for:

Today I learned:

_____

_____

_____

Date: _____

Today's Bible verse:

People in need of Prayer:

Prayer Requests:

Short term:

Long term:

Thank you Lord for:

Today I learned:

_____

_____

_____

Date: _____

Today's Bible verse:

People in need of Prayer:

Prayer Requests:

Short term:

Long term:

Thank you Lord for:

Today I learned:

_____

_____

_____

Date: _____

Today's Bible verse:	**People in need of Prayer:**

Prayer Requests:

Short term:

Long term:

Thank you Lord for:

Today I learned:

_____

_____

_____

Date: _____

Today's Bible verse:

People in need of Prayer:

Prayer Requests:

Short term:

Long term:

Thank you Lord for:

Today I learned:

_____

_____

_____

For this is the message
that ye heard from the
beginning, that we should
love one another.

1 John 3:11 (KJV)

Date: _____

Today's Bible verse:

People in need of Prayer:

Prayer Requests:

Short term:

Long term:

Thank you Lord for:

Today I learned:

_____

_____

_____

Date: _____

Today's Bible verse:

People in need of Prayer:

Prayer Requests:

Short term:

Long term:

Thank you Lord for:

Today I learned:

_____

_____

_____

Date: _____

Today's Bible verse:

People in need of Prayer:

Prayer Requests:

Short term:

Long term:

Thank you Lord for:

Today I learned:

_____

_____

_____

Date: _____

Today's Bible verse:

People in need of Prayer:

Prayer Requests:
Short term:

Long term:

Thank you Lord for:

Today I learned:

_____

_____

_____

Date: _____

Today's Bible verse:

People in need of Prayer:

Prayer Requests:

Short term:

Long term:

Thank you Lord for:

Today I learned:

_____

_____

_____

Date: _____

Today's Bible verse:

People in need of Prayer:

Prayer Requests:

Short term:

Long term:

Thank you Lord for:

Today I learned:

_____

_____

_____

Date: _____

Today's Bible verse:

People in need of Prayer:

Prayer Requests:

Short term:

Long term:

Thank you Lord for:

Today I learned:

_____

_____

_____

Date: _____

Today's Bible verse:

People in need of Prayer:

Prayer Requests:

Short term:

Long term:

Thank you Lord for:

Today I learned:

_____
_____
_____

Date: _____

Today's Bible verse:

People in need of Prayer:

Prayer Requests:

Short term:

Long term:

Thank you Lord for:

Today I learned:

_____

_____

_____

Date: _____

Today's Bible verse:

People in need of Prayer:

Prayer Requests:

Short term:

Long term:

Thank you Lord for:

Today I learned:

_____

_____

_____

Date: _____

Today's Bible verse:

People in need of Prayer:

Prayer Requests:

Short term:

Long term:

Thank you Lord for:

Today I learned:

_____

_____

_____

Date: _____

Today's Bible verse:

People in need of Prayer:

Prayer Requests:

Short term:

Long term:

Thank you Lord for:

Today I learned:

_____

_____

_____

Date: _____

Today's Bible verse:

People in need of Prayer:

Prayer Requests:

Short term:

Long term:

Thank you Lord for:

Today I learned:

_____
_____
_____

Date: _____

Today's Bible verse:

People in need of Prayer:

Prayer Requests:

Short term:

Long term:

Thank you Lord for:

Today I learned:

_____

_____

_____

Date: _____

Today's Bible verse:

People in need of Prayer:

Prayer Requests:

Short term:

Long term:

Thank you Lord for:

Today I learned:

_____

_____

_____

Date: _____

Today's Bible verse:

People in need of Prayer:

Prayer Requests:

Short term:

Long term:

Thank you Lord for:

Today I learned:

_____

_____

_____

Date: _____

Today's Bible verse:

People in need of Prayer:

Prayer Requests:

Short term:

Long term:

Thank you Lord for:

Today I learned:

_____

_____

_____

We love him, because he first loved us.

1 John 4:19 (KJV)

Date: _____

Today's Bible verse:

People in need of Prayer:

Prayer Requests:

Short term:

Long term:

Thank you Lord for:

Today I learned:

_____

_____

_____

Date: _____

Today's Bible verse:

People in need of Prayer:

Prayer Requests:

Short term:

Long term:

Thank you Lord for:

Today I learned:

_____

_____

_____

Date: _____

Today's Bible verse:

People in need of Prayer:

Prayer Requests:

Short term:

Long term:

Thank you Lord for:

Today I learned:

_____

_____

_____

Date: _____

Today's Bible verse:

People in need of Prayer:

Prayer Requests:

Short term:

Long term:

Thank you Lord for:

Today I learned:

_____
_____
_____

Date: _____

Today's Bible verse:

People in need of Prayer:

Prayer Requests:

Short term:

Long term:

Thank you Lord for:

Today I learned:

_____

_____

_____

Date: _____

Today's Bible verse:

People in need of Prayer:

Prayer Requests:

Short term:

Long term:

Thank you Lord for:

Today I learned:

_____

_____

_____

Date: _____

Today's Bible verse:

People in need of Prayer:

Prayer Requests:

Short term:

Long term:

Thank you Lord for:

Today I learned:

_____

_____

_____

Date: _____

Today's Bible verse:

People in need of Prayer:

Prayer Requests:
Short term:

Long term:

Thank you Lord for:

Today I learned:

_____

_____

_____

Date: _____

Today's Bible verse:

People in need of Prayer:

Prayer Requests:

Short term:

Long term:

Thank you Lord for:

Today I learned:

_____

_____

_____

Date: _____

Today's Bible verse:

People in need of Prayer:

Prayer Requests:

Short term:

Long term:

Thank you Lord for:

Today I learned:

_____

_____

_____

Date: _____

Today's Bible verse:

People in need of Prayer:

Prayer Requests:

Short term:

Long term:

Thank you Lord for:

Today I learned:

_____
_____
_____

Date: _____

Today's Bible verse:

People in need of Prayer:

Prayer Requests:

Short term:

Long term:

Thank you Lord for:

Today I learned:

_____

_____

_____

Date: _____

Today's Bible verse:

People in need of Prayer:

Prayer Requests:

Short term:

Long term:

Thank you Lord for:

Today I learned:

_____

_____

_____

Date: _____

Today's Bible verse:

People in need of Prayer:

Prayer Requests:

Short term:

Long term:

Thank you Lord for:

Today I learned:

_____

_____

_____

Date: _____

Today's Bible verse:

People in need of Prayer:

Prayer Requests:

Short term:

Long term:

Thank you Lord for:

Today I learned:

_____
_____
_____

Date: _____

Today's Bible verse:

People in need of Prayer:

Prayer Requests:

Short term:

Long term:

Thank you Lord for:

Today I learned:

_____
_____
_____

Date: _____

Today's Bible verse:

People in need of Prayer:

Prayer Requests:

Short term:

Long term:

Thank you Lord for:

Today I learned:

_____

_____

_____

This is the day which the
LORD hath made; we will
rejoice and be glad in it.

Psalm 118:24 (KJV)

Date: _____

Today's Bible verse:

People in need of Prayer:

Prayer Requests:

Short term:

Long term:

Thank you Lord for:

Today I learned:

_____
_____
_____

Date: _____

Today's Bible verse:

People in need of Prayer:

Prayer Requests:

Short term:

Long term:

Thank you Lord for:

Today I learned:

_____

_____

_____

Date: _____

Today's Bible verse:

People in need of Prayer:

Prayer Requests:

Short term:

Long term:

Thank you Lord for:

Today I learned:

_____

_____

_____

Date: _____

Today's Bible verse:

People in need of Prayer:

Prayer Requests:

Short term:

Long term:

Thank you Lord for:

Today I learned:

_____

_____

_____

Date: _____

Today's Bible verse:

People in need of Prayer:

Prayer Requests:

Short term:

Long term:

Thank you Lord for:

Today I learned:

_____

_____

_____

Date: _____

Today's Bible verse:

People in need of Prayer:

Prayer Requests:

Short term:

Long term:

Thank you Lord for:

Today I learned:

_____

_____

_____

Date: _____

Today's Bible verse:

People in need of Prayer:

Prayer Requests:

Short term:

Long term:

Thank you Lord for:

Today I learned:

_____

_____

_____

Date: _____

Today's Bible verse:

People in need of Prayer:

Prayer Requests:

Short term:

Long term:

Thank you Lord for:

Today I learned:

_____
_____
_____

Date: _____

Today's Bible verse:

People in need of Prayer:

Prayer Requests:

Short term:

Long term:

Thank you Lord for:

Today I learned:

_____
_____
_____

Date: _____

Today's Bible verse:

People in need of Prayer:

Prayer Requests:

Short term:

Long term:

Thank you Lord for:

Today I learned:

_____

_____

_____

Date: _____

Today's Bible verse:

People in need of Prayer:

Prayer Requests:

Short term:

Long term:

Thank you Lord for:

Today I learned:

_____

_____

_____

Date: _____

Today's Bible verse:

People in need of Prayer:

Prayer Requests:

Short term:

Long term:

Thank you Lord for:

Today I learned:

_____

_____

_____

Date: _____

Today's Bible verse:

People in need of Prayer:

Prayer Requests:

Short term:

Long term:

Thank you Lord for:

Today I learned:

_____
_____
_____

Date: _____

Today's Bible verse:

People in need of Prayer:

Prayer Requests:

Short term:

Long term:

Thank you Lord for:

Today I learned:

_____
_____
_____

Date: _____

Today's Bible verse:

People in need of Prayer:

Prayer Requests:

Short term:

Long term:

Thank you Lord for:

Today I learned:

_____

_____

_____

Date: _____

Today's Bible verse:

People in need of Prayer:

Prayer Requests:

Short term:

Long term:

Thank you Lord for:

Today I learned:

_____

_____

_____

Date: _____

Today's Bible verse:

People in need of Prayer:

Prayer Requests:

Short term:

Long term:

Thank you Lord for:

Today I learned:

_____
_____
_____

A Psalm of David. The
LORD is my shepherd;
I shall not want.

Psalm 23:1 (KJV)

Date: _____

Today's Bible verse:

People in need of Prayer:

Prayer Requests:

Short term:

Long term:

Thank you Lord for:

Today I learned:

_____
_____
_____

Date: _____

Today's Bible verse:

People in need of Prayer:

Prayer Requests:

Short term:

Long term:

Thank you Lord for:

Today I learned:

_____

_____

_____

Date: _____

Today's Bible verse:

People in need of Prayer:

Prayer Requests:

Short term:

Long term:

Thank you Lord for:

Today I learned:

_____

_____

_____

Date: _____

Today's Bible verse:

People in need of Prayer:

Prayer Requests:

Short term:

Long term:

Thank you Lord for:

Today I learned:

_____

_____

_____

Date: _____

Today's Bible verse:

People in need of Prayer:

Prayer Requests:

Short term:

Long term:

Thank you Lord for:

Today I learned:

_____

_____

_____

Date: _____

Today's Bible verse:

People in need of Prayer:

Prayer Requests:

Short term:

Long term:

Thank you Lord for:

Today I learned:

_____

_____

_____

Date: _____

Today's Bible verse:

People in need of Prayer:

Prayer Requests:

Short term:

Long term:

Thank you Lord for:

Today I learned:

_____
_____
_____

Date: _____

Today's Bible verse:

People in need of Prayer:

Prayer Requests:

Short term:

Long term:

Thank you Lord for:

Today I learned:

_____

_____

_____

Date: _____

Today's Bible verse:

People in need of Prayer:

Prayer Requests:

Short term:

Long term:

Thank you Lord for:

Today I learned:

_____
_____
_____

Date: _____

Today's Bible verse:

People in need of Prayer:

Prayer Requests:

Short term:

Long term:

Thank you Lord for:

Today I learned:

_____

_____

_____

Date: _____

Today's Bible verse:

People in need of Prayer:

Prayer Requests:

Short term:

Long term:

Thank you Lord for:

Today I learned:

_____

_____

_____

Date: _____

Today's Bible verse:

People in need of Prayer:

Prayer Requests:

Short term:

Long term:

Thank you Lord for:

Today I learned:

_____
_____
_____

Date: _____

Today's Bible verse:

People in need of Prayer:

Prayer Requests:

Short term:

Long term:

Thank you Lord for:

Today I learned:

_____
_____
_____

Date: _____

Today's Bible verse:

People in need of Prayer:

Prayer Requests:

Short term:

Long term:

Thank you Lord for:

Today I learned:

_____

_____

_____

Date: _____

Today's Bible verse:

People in need of Prayer:

Prayer Requests:

Short term:

Long term:

Thank you Lord for:

Today I learned:

_____

_____

_____

Date: _____

Today's Bible verse:

People in need of Prayer:

Prayer Requests:

Short term:

Long term:

Thank you Lord for:

Today I learned:

_____

_____

_____

Date: _____

Today's Bible verse:

People in need of Prayer:

Prayer Requests:

Short term:

Long term:

Thank you Lord for:

Today I learned:

_____

_____

_____

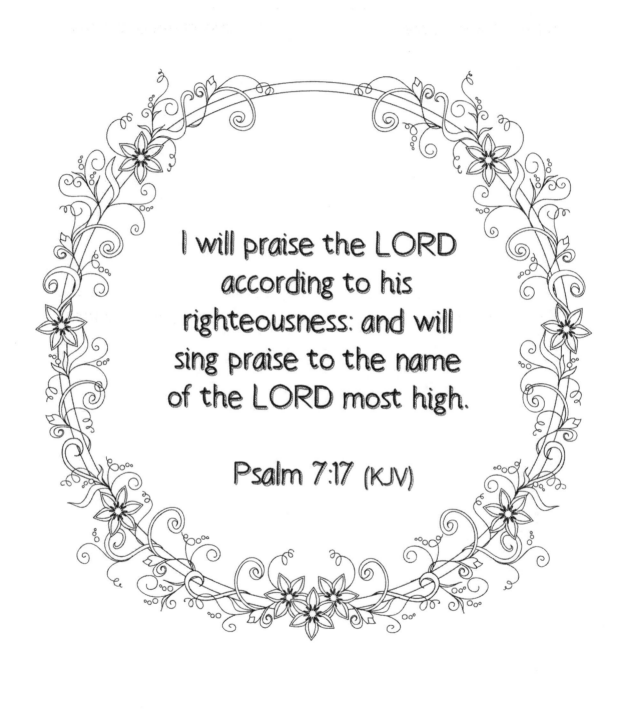

I will praise the LORD
according to his
righteousness: and will
sing praise to the name
of the LORD most high.

Psalm 7:17 (KJV)

Date: _____

Today's Bible verse:

People in need of Prayer:

Prayer Requests:

Short term:

Long term:

Thank you Lord for:

Today I learned:

_____

_____

_____

Date: _____

Today's Bible verse:

People in need of Prayer:

Prayer Requests:

Short term:

Long term:

Thank you Lord for:

Today I learned:

_____

_____

_____

Date: _____

Today's Bible verse:

People in need of Prayer:

Prayer Requests:

Short term:

Long term:

Thank you Lord for:

Today I learned:

_____

_____

_____

Date: _____

Today's Bible verse:

People in need of Prayer:

Prayer Requests:

Short term:

Long term:

Thank you Lord for:

Today I learned:

_____
_____
_____

Date: _____

Today's Bible verse:

People in need of Prayer:

Prayer Requests:

Short term:

Long term:

Thank you Lord for:

Today I learned:

_____

_____

_____

Date: _____

Today's Bible verse:

People in need of Prayer:

Prayer Requests:

Short term:

Long term:

Thank you Lord for:

Today I learned:

_____

_____

_____

Date: _____

Today's Bible verse:

People in need of Prayer:

Prayer Requests:

Short term:

Long term:

Thank you Lord for:

Today I learned:

_____

_____

_____

Date: _____

Today's Bible verse:

People in need of Prayer:

Prayer Requests:

Short term:

Long term:

Thank you Lord for:

Today I learned:

_____

_____

_____

Date: _____

Today's Bible verse:

People in need of Prayer:

Prayer Requests:

Short term:

Long term:

Thank you Lord for:

Today I learned:

_____

_____

_____

Date: _____

Today's Bible verse:

People in need of Prayer:

Prayer Requests:

Short term:

Long term:

Thank you Lord for:

Today I learned:

_____

_____

_____

Date: _____

Today's Bible verse:

People in need of Prayer:

Prayer Requests:

Short term:

Long term:

Thank you Lord for:

Today I learned:

_____
_____
_____

Date: _____

Today's Bible verse:

People in need of Prayer:

Prayer Requests:

Short term:

Long term:

Thank you Lord for:

Today I learned:

_____

_____

_____

Date: _____

Today's Bible verse:

People in need of Prayer:

Prayer Requests:

Short term:

Long term:

Thank you Lord for:

Today I learned:

_____

_____

_____

Date: _____

Today's Bible verse:

People in need of Prayer:

Prayer Requests:

Short term:

Long term:

Thank you Lord for:

Today I learned:

_____
_____
_____

Date: _____

Today's Bible verse:

People in need of Prayer:

Prayer Requests:

Short term:

Long term:

Thank you Lord for:

Today I learned:

_____

_____

_____

Date: _____

Today's Bible verse:

People in need of Prayer:

Prayer Requests:

Short term:

Long term:

Thank you Lord for:

Today I learned:

_____
_____
_____

Date: _____

Today's Bible verse:

People in need of Prayer:

Prayer Requests:

Short term:

Long term:

Thank you Lord for:

Today I learned:

_____
_____
_____

I can do all things through
Christ which
strengtheneth me.

Philippians 4:13 (KJV)

Date: _____

Today's Bible verse:

People in need of Prayer:

Prayer Requests:

Short term:

Long term:

Thank you Lord for:

Today I learned:

_____
_____
_____

Date: _____

Today's Bible verse:

People in need of Prayer:

Prayer Requests:

Short term:

Long term:

Thank you Lord for:

Today I learned:

_____
_____
_____

Date: _____

Today's Bible verse:

People in need of Prayer:

Prayer Requests:

Short term:

Long term:

Thank you Lord for:

Today I learned:

_____
_____
_____

Date: _____

Today's Bible verse:

People in need of Prayer:

Prayer Requests:

Short term:

Long term:

Thank you Lord for:

Today I learned:

_____
_____
_____

Date: _____

Today's Bible verse:

People in need of Prayer:

Prayer Requests:

Short term:

Long term:

Thank you Lord for:

Today I learned:

_____
_____
_____

Date: _____

Today's Bible verse:

People in need of Prayer:

Prayer Requests:

Short term:

Long term:

Thank you Lord for:

Today I learned:

_____

_____

_____

Date: _____

Today's Bible verse:

People in need of Prayer:

Prayer Requests:

Short term:

Long term:

Thank you Lord for:

Today I learned:

_____

_____

_____

Date: _____

Today's Bible verse:

People in need of Prayer:

Prayer Requests:

Short term:

Long term:

Thank you Lord for:

Today I learned:

_____
_____
_____

Date: _____

Today's Bible verse:

People in need of Prayer:

Prayer Requests:

Short term:

Long term:

Thank you Lord for:

Today I learned:

_____

_____

_____

Date: _____

Today's Bible verse:

People in need of Prayer:

Prayer Requests:

Short term:

Long term:

Thank you Lord for:

Today I learned:

_____

_____

_____

Date: _____

Today's Bible verse:

People in need of Prayer:

Prayer Requests:

Short term:

Long term:

Thank you Lord for:

Today I learned:

_____

_____

_____

Date: _____

Today's Bible verse:

People in need of Prayer:

Prayer Requests:

Short term:

Long term:

Thank you Lord for:

Today I learned:

_____

_____

_____

Date: _____

Today's Bible verse:

People in need of Prayer:

Prayer Requests:

Short term:

Long term:

Thank you Lord for:

Today I learned:

_____

_____

_____

Date: _____

Today's Bible verse:

People in need of Prayer:

Prayer Requests:

Short term:

Long term:

Thank you Lord for:

Today I learned:

_____

_____

_____

Date: _____

Today's Bible verse:

People in need of Prayer:

Prayer Requests:

Short term:

Long term:

Thank you Lord for:

Today I learned:

_____

_____

_____

Date: _____

Today's Bible verse:	People in need of Prayer:

Prayer Requests:

Short term:

Long term:

Thank you Lord for:

Today I learned:

_____

_____

_____

Date: _____

Today's Bible verse:

People in need of Prayer:

Prayer Requests:

Short term:

Long term:

Thank you Lord for:

Today I learned:

_____

_____

_____

O give thanks unto the LORD, for he is good: for his mercy endureth for ever.

Psalm 107:1 (KJV)

Date: _____

Today's Bible verse:

People in need of Prayer:

Prayer Requests:

Short term:

Long term:

Thank you Lord for:

Today I learned:

_____

_____

_____

Date: _____

Today's Bible verse:

People in need of Prayer:

Prayer Requests:

Short term:

Long term:

Thank you Lord for:

Today I learned:

_____

_____

_____

Date: _____

Today's Bible verse:

People in need of Prayer:

Prayer Requests:

Short term:

Long term:

Thank you Lord for:

Today I learned:

_____

_____

_____

Date: _____

Today's Bible verse:

People in need of Prayer:

Prayer Requests:

Short term:

Long term:

Thank you Lord for:

Today I learned:

_____

_____

_____

Date: _____

Today's Bible verse:

People in need of Prayer:

Prayer Requests:

Short term:

Long term:

Thank you Lord for:

Today I learned:

_____

_____

_____

Date: _____

Today's Bible verse:

People in need of Prayer:

Prayer Requests:

Short term:

Long term:

Thank you Lord for:

Today I learned:

_____

_____

_____

Date: _____

Today's Bible verse:

People in need of Prayer:

Prayer Requests:

Short term:

Long term:

Thank you Lord for:

Today I learned:

_____

_____

_____

Date: _____

Today's Bible verse:

People in need of Prayer:

Prayer Requests:

Short term:

Long term:

Thank you Lord for:

Today I learned:

_____

_____

_____

Date: _____

Today's Bible verse:

People in need of Prayer:

Prayer Requests:

Short term:

Long term:

Thank you Lord for:

Today I learned:

_____

_____

_____

Date: _____

Today's Bible verse:

People in need of Prayer:

Prayer Requests:
Short term:

Long term:

Thank you Lord for:

Today I learned:

_____
_____
_____

Date: _____

Today's Bible verse:

People in need of Prayer:

Prayer Requests:

Short term:

Long term:

Thank you Lord for:

Today I learned:

_____

_____

_____

Date: _____

Today's Bible verse:

People in need of Prayer:

Prayer Requests:

Short term:

Long term:

Thank you Lord for:

Today I learned:

_____

_____

_____

Date: _____

Today's Bible verse:

People in need of Prayer:

Prayer Requests:

Short term:

Long term:

Thank you Lord for:

Today I learned:

_____
_____
_____

Date: _____

Today's Bible verse:

People in need of Prayer:

Prayer Requests:

Short term:

Long term:

Thank you Lord for:

Today I learned:

_____

_____

_____

Date: _____

Today's Bible verse:

People in need of Prayer:

Prayer Requests:

Short term:

Long term:

Thank you Lord for:

Today I learned:

_____

_____

_____

Date: _____

Today's Bible verse:	People in need of Prayer:

Prayer Requests:	Thank you Lord for:
Short term:	
Long term:	

Today I learned:

_____

_____

_____

Date: _____

Today's Bible verse:

People in need of Prayer:

Prayer Requests:

Short term:

Long term:

Thank you Lord for:

Today I learned:

_____

_____

_____

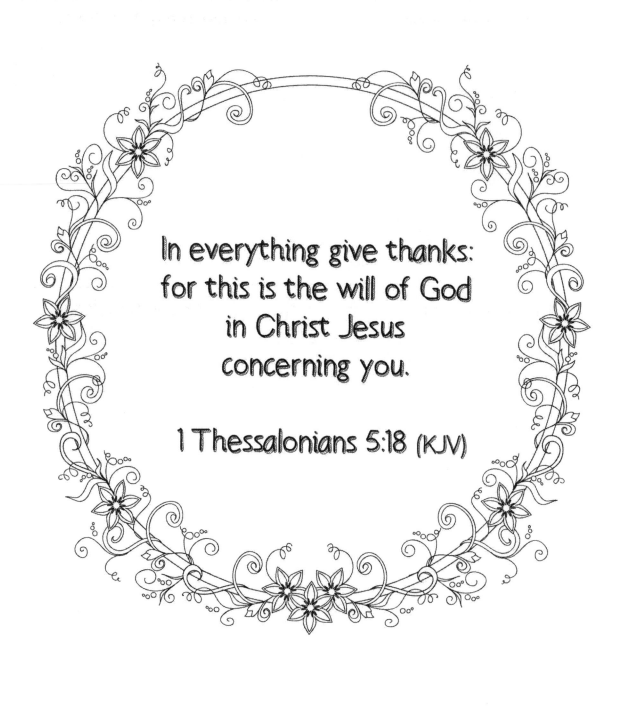

In everything give thanks:
for this is the will of God
in Christ Jesus
concerning you.

1 Thessalonians 5:18 (KJV)

Date: _____

Today's Bible verse:

People in need of Prayer:

Prayer Requests:

Short term:

Long term:

Thank you Lord for:

Today I learned:

_____

_____

_____

Date: _____

Today's Bible verse:

People in need of Prayer:

Prayer Requests:

Short term:

Long term:

Thank you Lord for:

Today I learned:

_____

_____

_____

Date: _____

Today's Bible verse:

People in need of Prayer:

Prayer Requests:

Short term:

Long term:

Thank you Lord for:

Today I learned:

_____

_____

_____

Date: _____

Today's Bible verse:

People in need of Prayer:

Prayer Requests:
Short term:

Long term:

Thank you Lord for:

Today I learned:

_____

_____

_____

Date: _____

Today's Bible verse:

People in need of Prayer:

Prayer Requests:

Short term:

Long term:

Thank you Lord for:

Today I learned:

_____

_____

_____

Date: _____

Today's Bible verse:

People in need of Prayer:

Prayer Requests:

Short term:

Long term:

Thank you Lord for:

Today I learned:

_____

_____

_____

Date: _____

Today's Bible verse:

People in need of Prayer:

Prayer Requests:

Short term:

Long term:

Thank you Lord for:

Today I learned:

_____

_____

_____

Date: _____

Today's Bible verse:

People in need of Prayer:

Prayer Requests:

Short term:

Long term:

Thank you Lord for:

Today I learned:

_____

_____

_____

Date: _____

Today's Bible verse:

People in need of Prayer:

Prayer Requests:

Short term:

Long term:

Thank you Lord for:

Today I learned:

_____

_____

_____

Date: _____

Today's Bible verse:

People in need of Prayer:

Prayer Requests:

Short term:

Long term:

Thank you Lord for:

Today I learned:

_____

_____

_____

Date: _____

Today's Bible verse:

People in need of Prayer:

Prayer Requests:

Short term:

Long term:

Thank you Lord for:

Today I learned:

_____

_____

_____

Date: _____

Today's Bible verse:

People in need of Prayer:

Prayer Requests:

Short term:

Long term:

Thank you Lord for:

Today I learned:

_____

_____

_____

Date: _____

Today's Bible verse:

People in need of Prayer:

Prayer Requests:

Short term:

Long term:

Thank you Lord for:

Today I learned:

_____

_____

_____

Date: _____

Today's Bible verse:

People in need of Prayer:

Prayer Requests:

Short term:

Long term:

Thank you Lord for:

Today I learned:

_____

_____

_____

Date: _____

Today's Bible verse:

People in need of Prayer:

Prayer Requests:

Short term:

Long term:

Thank you Lord for:

Today I learned:

_____

_____

_____

Date: _____

Today's Bible verse:

People in need of Prayer:

Prayer Requests:

Short term:

Long term:

Thank you Lord for:

Today I learned:

_____
_____
_____

Date: _____

Today's Bible verse:

People in need of Prayer:

Prayer Requests:

Short term:

Long term:

Thank you Lord for:

Today I learned:

_____

_____

_____

Be still, and know that
I am God.

Psalm 46:10 (KJV)

Date: _____

Today's Bible verse:

People in need of Prayer:

Prayer Requests:

Short term:

Long term:

Thank you Lord for:

Today I learned:

_____

_____

_____

Date: _____

Today's Bible verse:

People in need of Prayer:

Prayer Requests:

Short term:

Long term:

Thank you Lord for:

Today I learned:

_____

_____

_____

Date: _____

Today's Bible verse:

People in need of Prayer:

Prayer Requests:

Short term:

Long term:

Thank you Lord for:

Today I learned:

_____

_____

_____

Date: _____

Today's Bible verse:

People in need of Prayer:

Prayer Requests:

Short term:

Long term:

Thank you Lord for:

Today I learned:

_____
_____
_____

Date: _____

Today's Bible verse:

People in need of Prayer:

Prayer Requests:

Short term:

Long term:

Thank you Lord for:

Today I learned:

_____

_____

_____

Date: _____

Today's Bible verse:

People in need of Prayer:

Prayer Requests:

Short term:

Long term:

Thank you Lord for:

Today I learned:

_____

_____

_____

Date: _____

Today's Bible verse:

People in need of Prayer:

Prayer Requests:

Short term:

Long term:

Thank you Lord for:

Today I learned:

_____

_____

_____

Date: _____

Today's Bible verse:

People in need of Prayer:

Prayer Requests:

Short term:

Long term:

Thank you Lord for:

Today I learned:

_____

_____

_____

Date: _____

Today's Bible verse:

People in need of Prayer:

Prayer Requests:

Short term:

Long term:

Thank you Lord for:

Today I learned:

_____

_____

_____

Date: _____

Today's Bible verse:

People in need of Prayer:

Prayer Requests:

Short term:

Long term:

Thank you Lord for:

Today I learned:

_____

_____

_____

Date: _____

Today's Bible verse:

People in need of Prayer:

Prayer Requests:

Short term:

Long term:

Thank you Lord for:

Today I learned:

_____

_____

_____

Date: _____

Today's Bible verse:

People in need of Prayer:

Prayer Requests:

Short term:

Long term:

Thank you Lord for:

Today I learned:

_____

_____

_____

Date: _____

Today's Bible verse:

People in need of Prayer:

Prayer Requests:

Short term:

Long term:

Thank you Lord for:

Today I learned:

_____

_____

_____

Date: _____

Today's Bible verse:	People in need of Prayer:

Prayer Requests:

Short term:

Long term:

Thank you Lord for:

Today I learned:

_____

_____

_____

Date: _____

Today's Bible verse:

People in need of Prayer:

Prayer Requests:

Short term:

Long term:

Thank you Lord for:

Today I learned:

_____
_____
_____

Date: _____

Today's Bible verse:

People in need of Prayer:

Prayer Requests:

Short term:

Long term:

Thank you Lord for:

Today I learned:

_____
_____
_____

Date: _____

Today's Bible verse:

People in need of Prayer:

Prayer Requests:

Short term:

Long term:

Thank you Lord for:

Today I learned:

_____

_____

_____

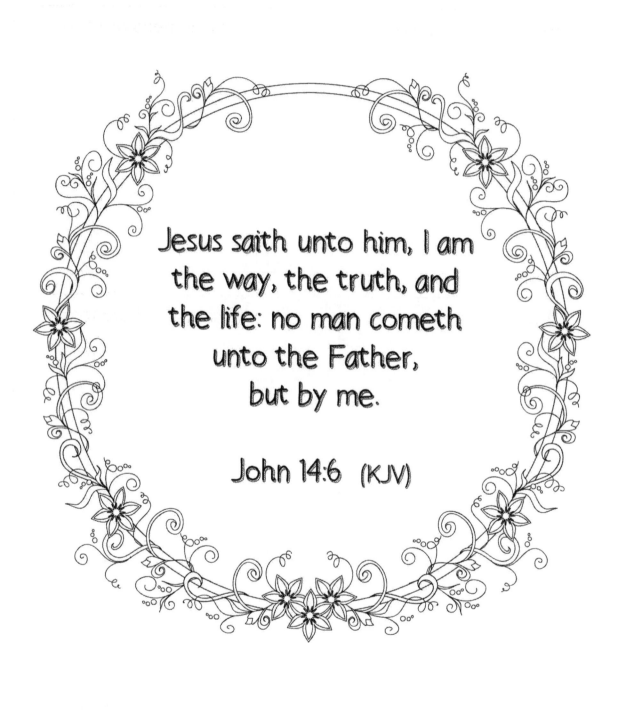

Jesus saith unto him, I am
the way, the truth, and
the life: no man cometh
unto the Father,
but by me.

John 14:6 (KJV)

Date: _____

Today's Bible verse:

People in need of Prayer:

Prayer Requests:

Short term:

Long term:

Thank you Lord for:

Today I learned:

_____

_____

_____

Date: _____

Today's Bible verse:

People in need of Prayer:

Prayer Requests:

Short term:

Long term:

Thank you Lord for:

Today I learned:

_____

_____

_____

Date: _____

Today's Bible verse:

People in need of Prayer:

Prayer Requests:

Short term:

Long term:

Thank you Lord for:

Today I learned:

_____
_____
_____

Date: _____

Today's Bible verse:

People in need of Prayer:

Prayer Requests:

Short term:

Long term:

Thank you Lord for:

Today I learned:

_____
_____
_____

Date: _____

<table>
<tr><td>

Today's Bible verse:

</td><td>

People in need of Prayer:

</td></tr>
<tr><td>

Prayer Requests:

Short term:

Long term:

</td><td>

Thank you Lord for:

</td></tr>
</table>

Today I learned:

_____

_____

_____

Date: _____

Today's Bible verse:

People in need of Prayer:

Prayer Requests:

Short term:

Long term:

Thank you Lord for:

Today I learned:

_____

_____

_____

Date: _____

Today's Bible verse:

People in need of Prayer:

Prayer Requests:

Short term:

Long term:

Thank you Lord for:

Today I learned:

_____

_____

_____

Date: _____

Today's Bible verse:

People in need of Prayer:

Prayer Requests:

Short term:

Long term:

Thank you Lord for:

Today I learned:

_____

_____

_____

Date: _____

Today's Bible verse:

People in need of Prayer:

Prayer Requests:

Short term:

Long term:

Thank you Lord for:

Today I learned:

_____

_____

_____

Date: _____

Today's Bible verse:

People in need of Prayer:

Prayer Requests:

Short term:

Long term:

Thank you Lord for:

Today I learned:

_____

_____

_____

Date: _____

Today's Bible verse:

People in need of Prayer:

Prayer Requests:

Short term:

Long term:

Thank you Lord for:

Today I learned:

_____
_____
_____

Date: _____

Today's Bible verse:

People in need of Prayer:

Prayer Requests:

Short term:

Long term:

Thank you Lord for:

Today I learned:

_____

_____

_____

Made in the USA
Columbia, SC
14 December 2018